Urban Transparencies

Also by Mark Willing and published by Ginninderra Press
Spirit Level

Mark Willing

Urban Transparencies

Urban Transparencies
ISBN 978 1 74027 810 2
Copyright © Mark Willing 2013
Cover photo © WONG SZE FEI - Fotolia.com

First published 2013
Reprinted 2017

GINNINDERRA PRESS
PO Box 3461 Port Adelaide SA 5015
www.ginninderrapress.com.au

Contents

The Hut	7
Beneath	8
The Emptiness	9
Horizon	11
Thinking In Light	12
Closing In Beyond Evidence	13
Waving At Italy	14
Barista Spirit	15
The Disgraceful Life of Kettles	16
Chocolate	18
Archie Harbison	19
Humans In the Mist	20
Royal Image – Canberra	21
Eleven	22
Quiet Companion	23
Mattresses On Nature Strips	24
Dance Hall Days	25
Terror Mountain	26
Ella's Shadow	28
Bareback Canticles	29
Things My Children May Have Found	30
Incline	31
4 a.m.	33
The Pointy End	34
Urban Transparencies	36
Kevin's Infection	38
The Kitchen	39
Monk Who Prays So Much…	41
Ways To Approach the Kingdom	42
Fear In a Handful of Dust	44

Wet Salvage Auto Waste	45
Plum Tree	48
Comfort	49
No Moon Dark	50
The Scarred Tree	51
Magpie	53
Ceremony Poems	54
At the Homecoming Conference For Philosophers	57
Burying	58
The Solitary Boat	59
The Painting	60
Terra Momentum	61
Growing Old	63
Mutating Contours of a Lime Sea	64
A Long, Low-sweeping Pastoral Sadness	65
Filling the Gaps	69
The Immensity	70
Farmhouse	72

The Hut

Above the hut
a lithograph of stars.
Inside, a stick broom sweeps the earth.
In a corner the youngest girl
bathes the baby.
At the table the father
sorts merchandise for the neighbours.
On goatskin the eldest girl
reads a book of fabled histories.
On the stone bench the son
cleans an old rifle for war.
Beneath the only window
a jug of earthen colours
holds water from a well
dug centuries ago.
Above the thatched roof
a mother lode of stars
illuminates the hut
with its solitary lamp.

Beneath

Marina, in the smoky chaos
are you fumed to igniting
do you sleep well

are you shaping your pact
your final rendezvous
sharp as an arctic sliver

is your heart leathered up
to beat back the years
of too much ice in your veins

how many dull-eyed youths
weigh now upon your breasts

in all the conundrum of progress
since you left the door open

do you forgive
as one who lies beneath
the unforgiving snow?

The Emptiness

At the end of our street
there used to be a deep cutting
where the storm water spilled out.
It had a concrete overpass
with loose scuttling rock edges
falling away to a dark recess below.

The local kids all called it The Emptiness.
We were warned about the dangers
how if we go there we might not come back
so we spent most of our loose hours there.

One day Kevin Harbison went there alone.
He didn't come back for six months
and when he did
he had a long scar
down the side of his skull
and talked out of the corner of his mouth.
We never really knew Kevin after that.

Driving back to the street
where I used to live
I remembered The Emptiness.
It had all been filled in
with a housing estate on top.

Children were playing on well-kept lawns.
Families and cars were coming and going.
I remembered the stranger
who had been standing on the overpass
who said he'd never seen so much blood.

I didn't know him.
I didn't know Kevin Harbison.
I didn't know any of these people.
But I remembered The Emptiness.

Horizon

Outward from a high railing over the immense ferocity of a southern ocean, a moment of visitation of an anthemic ghostlike hum
Sudden explosions of white noise, angelic chords, infinite swell and tide
The vision erupts and as quickly collapses into an intense sparking icon drifting in the air above
Radiant pulsations of arc light implode, bounce off themselves, cannoning between earth and sky, then explode into the most dazzling array
Over it all, the electrified air, the ultimate of all light, we see him pacing his horizon, we see him in vertical streams of blinding fission, we see him in the atomic fields of the sun
We see him even through this light as if illuminated by a stronger source that is light from his own hand
We see him there as if it is his time to flow out over all earth and all heavens, we see him and feel his power of creation around and within
As one, only one.

Thinking In Light

Searching for an address where we actually think in poetry
not language, where speech and thought become plainchant
for the cursive sprawl of arboreal mindscapes and not just
inherited syntax.
Crossing St Kilda Road from the National Gallery
we come into parklands towards a spreading elm
a picture of colonial wilderness symmetry
its angles and planes shifting between great shade and the
heat of noon
the smell of summer grass rising up
a depth of lucent music in the business of insects
as it would have been for tribal members before this tree was
planted.
Skittish dragonflies, birds sailing on repose
all things in light, wilfully reactive.
Transparent swarms searching the sky above.
Dreamt migrations brushing closed eyes.
Illumination, flight and the drumming of feet.
Thoughts and words escaping, redefining
assembling purpose in another dimension.
In the distance tall structures
mechanical exactness
precise light towers
for the wayward and the ill at ease.
In the elm a chanting of bees
swarming in perfect unison –
Gregorian by voice and intent.

Closing In Beyond Evidence

Closing in beyond evidence
a sheer delight in an opening volume
pages crisp from the night's cold breath

and that smell, parchment oiled
smearing its fine layer of song
over your wanting hands

wanting to touch and be touched
dancing between the words and lines
with promises not to pass through

gathering the scales of the serpent myth
flung for centuries about the fertile garden
richer than fruit on a swaying vine

the facts are carefully sealed
taken away in see-through skin
caressed with each flinch of an eye.

Waving At Italy

Scuttling in a godless sea
in a drowning theatre
of Mediterranean immensity

the form too souped up
the plot too thickened
for any dramatic acrobatic segue

into flailing democracies in a paper sky
raining flame on the orator
in a blur of momentum.

Unexpectedly the coast appears
a green line of survivors
hardly moving

then setting out in wafer flotillas
the way Romans did
before miracles became law.

Barista Spirit

Grinding it out of the grounds in the earth
from a flat hand spooned into a lid
then tossed by gravity into a tin cup.
Centripetal by law the hot water breathes
infusing drip by drip its aromatic draw
into the runners and leaves of exotic abundance.
Essence gives us all that we need
and in our addiction to need, essence restores
the true invention from the sieve of necessity.
Essence, then less than essence
our instinctual grip for less not more
like writers sitting around an inn table
counting out beans, culling parables
perfectly aligning their whiff of a good drop
with that sense of story
and the watery swell of pasty mystique
the steam rising, visible
then invisible.

The Disgraceful Life of Kettles

Not too many in their prime
or fresh in appearance
cornered in factory back rooms

grimed and greased
fingerprinted
even cobwebbed

steam fizzing
from cracks
in the joinery

crazed plastic bubbles
'on' switches dropped off
frayed poor aunts
of the electric age

provider of the instant
granule gratification
caffeine's plasticky
whore

still
the old boilers
go and go and go

searing their skin
to flaky
brittleness

until one day
seemingly they burn out
boil dry

nothing inside
but still waters.

Chocolate

Thinking of her
he watches her undress
and lean sideways across the doona.
Thinking of her he asks her if she wants a drink.
No, she says, I've got chocolate, love chocolate, mmm.
Sweet he says and puts the required amount delicately under
her purse.
Sweet she mocks then they're over here and over there
in an awful flurry of hair arms tongues swearing and grunts
and a doctor on the TV's proclaiming the benefits of daily
exercise
and he hears her somewhere in there give a little giggle
and twitch in the plastic plasma nervy nirvana
like the news coming on when you're not expecting it.
Thinking of her
he buries deeper than hibernation
counts the rings around the stars he keeps seeing
bites the lip of the ugliest woman on earth
until the gates wobble a little then crack
and she's already got more chocolate in her mouth
and he asks her her name
and she says I think you know I'm her.

Archie Harbison

Saw it coming, almost happen
through a rage of family dysfunction
in dusty banal forecasts
no rain for three years
the relentless blue of his eyes
canopied the lashed-out dramas
living in hope
the worm may turn overnight
with a clap of thunder
waking him from the noose-tight
embrace of his dreams
a last minute thought before sleeping
sounding like a thud on the roof
syllables of Mallee, Wimmera
the ones we learned in school
stomping down in rocky ferocity
like Harbison twins
lying low
in their dustbowl
of knuckle and last straw.

Humans In the Mist

(after Ambam, the upright gorilla)

Common trust and empathy cannot be too commonly assumed.
The silverback, frosty in faint English sunlight
draws himself up and walks on two legs.
Autocracy, not monarchy, brings him to a new food tier
his staunch body swaying in paper-thin mist
like a first human plodding the mud banks of the Thames
not yet thinking about any circle of governance
as a Westminster system of revolving argument.
He is the sole curator of his species
definition of his breed's impulsive truth
driven by action preceding reward.
He surveys the cameras blinding him with light
with the knowledge he has moved on
and with a lope away toward the border
he leaves them behind
in their canopies, their trucks, their darkness
searching in his escape for
their own evolutionary freedom.

Royal Image – Canberra

On Burley Griffin, the rough law
of monarchy pale-handedly
round-headedly receptive, resting on an oar
now rising from a summer frock
almost pure white cotton
to wave, not drowning.
For a second
something was thought to flutter
above the Duke's head, but the sky
was a clear October blue
and there was no time for shade.
Out on the water
they looked almost ant-like
and ever so slightly
rocking back and forth
with that motion of old age
dreamily, sleepily, almost
as if lineage was drifting.
Above, king parrots flew
into a royal blue firmament.

Eleven

Eleven years old.
I am in a yard
alone and facing the plum tree.
The tree is in one corner near the old garden shed.
I am crouching in the opposite corner.
Eugene and I are sitting in the branches
tasting the sweetest summer of our lives
T-shirts stained with juice
laughter traded like discarded piths
across the daring spaciousness of the huge tree.
We look down at the scene below.
I look up from the shadows.
Eugene has gone to Canada.
I'll see you no more blood brother.
But for now I focus on the tree.
I run towards it as fast as I can
until just before it I release my body
and let it cannon between sky and earth
until everything blackens in numb surrender.
Later, I feel my fingers running through fibres
of earth where something is beating
where all things, once spoken
will never be the same.

Quiet Companion

I am seeking the shelter of a shadow
in this late Indian summer.
Not the type you find under a house
with its cobwebs, mice and old paintings.
Nor a tree that spreads itself
in a kind embrace around the heat of noon.
Time is drawing close
when there will be only shadow
and I have embraced my children
for that one important tree-felling moment.
I have set them free
from mourning and uncertainty.
There is a quiet assurance these days
when daylight is waning
and shadows are all around.
There is a quiet companion arriving
and in these final words
in the shadow of his presence
I can say at last
I am here.
Count me in.

Mattresses On Nature Strips

Twisted like Dali clocks
around eucalypt branches, kitchen appliances
sprouting modern technology for old

they zig-zag up and down
some contorted
some defiled where they land
a complex trail of Oedipus
snaking along the edge of the roadway

can't help thinking
as you drive quickly by
or walk the dog past, dragging it away
marriages laid to rest
pubescent dreams gone up in smoke
stripped, dragged out, soaked into the ionosphere

don't go there
but if you do
be warned of illicit dealing
inner spring, foam or simply stuffed
the sag is the same, burden or impression

of all the hard waste passed on that way
these are the stuff of dream order
the unconscious, the netherworld, the lie.

Dance Hall Days

Clack-clack of stilettoed echo
perfection of promenade
empty now
a mollusc mustiness
of air and decadent sweat

shadows of silent pirouette
eating in where music blooms
like tick or tock
rhythms lagging over fads and fashions
joins with wallpaper thinness peeling
in the slant of gold-dust sunlit evenings

blinds flapped static,
only echoes remain
and an odd chair submersed
into auburn-burned panelling

once foxtrot, two-step, free-form release
now shimmers in the floating haze
of spacious chivalry, dance hall days
when a hand, ghostlike, emerging from oakwood
bows in grace to take you dancing

against the light
into the light.

Terror Mountain

Terror Mountain.
We're driving along its winding anorexic vein.
Inside the Austin, four of us cling-wrapped
using our arms as windshield wipers
besotted with choruses of 'How Great Thou Art'.
Outside the cool mountain air shivers through others
going about their raking, shopping or business deals.
We pass a church, the car goes quiet.
We pass another car over the white line
with big-dipper screams all round.
'What a Friend We Have In Jesus'
rides us all the way to Picnic Point
and a rug spread wide across scorch marks
from last summer's fires.
He'd gone away four days back then
fire fighting in the ranges
and we never thought we'd see him
until that flash dollar note
bristling and wax-smooth
was plunged into my ten-shilling palm.
She never gave up on him –
not forgotten, just never thought of –
and he drifted back and forth
fuelling the grit in her teeth and eyes.
Scones on a tin lid, jam in a cup
a game of French cricket
and my brother's natural round arm toss
of a lure into a muddy creek
gone before you could count to ten –
the number of fingers to hold a man down.

Those days, the eucalypt drift
the bark sailing down
around our rug
and the fog creeping in
and up the mountain and over the ridge
like the frozen breath of something arriving
from hymnals of laughter and fear.

Ella's Shadow

They are circling now. They are bringing her in.

They are bringing in another ship of human endeavour
around the heads through a wicked bombora
with white spray and pink balloons
kicking up a mighty entrance.

Sydney is all scorn with a wry smile
tucked in every nook
like daylight New Year's Eve
as they come down, as they spread out

parents and children with blankets and picnics
trying to make sense of a lesson in courage
persistence, endurance or the dogged rite
of someone who just knows her stuff.

They all wave, they all catch a glimpse
then head back to their homes
fathers with arms around daughters
and for a moment the fissure slightly narrows

for a moment, Australia breathes a sigh of relief
for a moment, she remembers
her shadow on the water
keeping up at a rate of knots

and beside it another she didn't know
circling, circling, bringing her in
like something she can't explain
but will be done.

Bareback Canticles

Overlapping choruses of 'tea's ready' and 'time to come home'
in the gathering dark of a suburban street
my brother with halter in hand, whispering gently
as the neighbourhood gang stoop down and lift up
as one body, the last of them to have a go.
The horse, one of many he would lead
through the winding tracks of his life
standing politely until nervous balance is maintained
then with slow dressage gait across shod-echoing bitumen
to where paddocks with rabbits are still the norm in a city.
Squeals and laughter make no impression on temperament.
Bareback canticles of 'giddup' and 'whoa boy'
having no more impact than wild west imagination.
After the last has alighted with excitement diminishing down the street
I watch his eyes as he knots his ropes
brushing broad-flanked sinew and changing the water
his eyes entering those equine subtleties with a deep knowing vast and
timeless.
I flick his braces and he comes round
as if being hoisted up out of one of his readings
in Latin or Greek, as if there is time for another go before he leaves
forever. Scholarships and hypotheses already whispering his name.
Time to leave home, to turn wild that ride
beyond his rope and rein.

Things My Children May Have Found

Sparkless catherine wheels
a seed pod of no consequence
a rusting box of screwdrivers next to a foundation
sketches of eyes all over a drawing pad and on the back of old bills
a piece of cloud stuffing gummed to a sky-coloured handkerchief
a poster of a nursery rhyme now unrhymed in a drawer
records with sleeves swapped to disguise the lack of cool
a note addressed to you
telling where devotion began
where nothing ended.

Incline

I am about to find out
what it was like back then.

Were you coy?
Had your streams begun linking arms?

I have a memory –
a trail of reddish earth
that zigzagged down a sharp incline
from the old railway cutting at the back of our school
cut into the clay over decades of rainwater
washing down to the suburb below.

It was our base camp
where we drew tattoos on our arms
hid bottle tops under rocks
and spoke venomously of girls.

Although dangerous, everyone used it as a shortcut
yet nobody fathomed its secondary life.

To this day, red earth and slippery inclines
feet gathering momentum, stomping for balance
the descent of horses, Snowy River legends
all bring back memories of the steep incline.

It was our Gallipoli where we played for keeps
its red sticky scree forever attached to our skins

but for now I'm still waiting for that clay taste of you
the one when you discovered my stash of bottle tops
and when you showed us how girls do real tattoos
with a sharp stick and blood.

I'm waiting to see you on the steep incline
your loose-hipped climb gathering mass upstream

waiting to see you
before you flowed.

4 a.m.

Sometimes I am blessed
in the lone company of this hour
in its beginning and in its end.
Sometimes, brushing over,
I feel the lesion
just above the ear
or the lump in the armpit
and then that old familiar
song of the sea
palpitation out of sync
with the lyre.
Sometimes it's the flash
just before sleep
waking me around 4 a.m.
to write it down
and then wait
for the sun to rise
on another of those lucky days
with gold light, music
fur, words and coffee.
Sometimes I could live
for the hour before dawn
forever.

The Pointy End

Looking up into his top-paddock sky
in 1912 he probably was thinking
maybe/maybe not, the rains/the dry.
One season to the next was all he could fathom
and beyond that, broad plains of learnt and instinctual
never more than a toss of a coin or die.
Whatever lay beyond was outside his realm of reason.
Simple luxuries – a collection of hats in pegged rows
broad-brimmed/peaked, Sunday/weekday
tools in the lean-to, earth-stained/sapped
and opinions tucked into subdivided patterns
of how he wished/hoped/dreamed in phrases
not yet ingrained into a sentenced landscape.
Looking up in one of those rare, lazed intermissions
between sowing and harvest of his scored sense of place
a man of philosophies in his escapades of knowledge
strolling alongside the silent language of horses
or raising the freshwater plimsoll to his ankles
brought down from rivers of the zigzag huons
where some blight had crossed blades in the spring.
By his reckoning there would be no Collins Street farm law
come close to entering beyond his fenceline
no taxes, no grants, no future drought-proofing
of where we've become assured through programmed assurance
and the laser-red models of each next disaster
whether flood/drought, bushfire/stagnation
the pointy end of agrarian expertise
governments who hold sway over good faith in the season
cut-to-the-chase mongers of scare and futility
policies as pagan as masks of fertility.

By his reckoning, looking up from his 1912 paddock
there could be tomorrow before it rains
maybe/maybe not.

Urban Transparencies

All over creation it seemed
rain was falling from a grey gut
plethora of cloudburst, palimpsest of binge

Across all scriptures of flood
be it rooftop or water tank
gorge or wheel rut.

All over the crown of trees
in their deepest foliaged slumber
ariels hummed with faint recognitions.

Threads of distant rites of passage
sliced delicately through
these urban transparencies

Dipping into puddles
like a treasure box of fortune
only to see themselves and laugh in fright

Only to bear witness
under greatcoat skies
shadowing the outside world.

All over our lives it seemed
there were always obligatories
snapped shut into hourglasses and small packages
of phobias, of nightmares, of those things
least expected to tell truths in the dark.

All over all we believed in
came winged and hoofed shapes
upon our childish horizons
and we bowed, contorted ourselves
but could never avoid the rain.

Sometimes, through the night lattice
we could sense it by the way
pieces of the outside world
would flick and curl
under the scraping weight
of the infinite.

Kevin's Infection

Kevin wading in trousers rolled up to the knees
his back stooped pointing the Sunday night camera lens of
current, not past, affairs
down a river of street chattels, wheelie bins filled with
clothes, floating banana lounges
piles of debris on nature strips, roads and front yards merging
into a utopian, socially equitable body of earthen water.
Here Kevin points to some student quarters.
They're away in Phuket and he's taken it upon himself
to carry their belongings to higher ground.
Kevin in a socially expressive free world
where anything goes whether by title or by name
even in the same line in the same lineage of style
or, as Keating might have pronounced
where there is no suffering, because it is all suffering.
Meanwhile, back to Kevin carrying whole pianos on his back
pants now rolled up to dangerously high levels.
Kevin, pointing teary-eyed at this family and that
squatting gob-smacked on tin roofs.
Kevin's infection grows over the next two weeks.
He carries its raw poultice of Queensland sugar cane
to Egypt where the back-stabbing continues, making Kevin
smile secretly.
Panadol and Rawleigh's antiseptic salve can't prevent every
malaise.
Kevin, like so many fellow citizens, beaten to a pulp
infected beyond his loyal streak
wading through the rising level of snakes, vipers
and the occasional floating crap.

The Kitchen

In the kitchen of the Californian bungalow
even the jagged cracks opening up
in the lath and plaster of the walls and their shadows
even there, where light is fear unto itself
there is a lemon-tinctured glow all about the room
where we are singing, whirling, dancing
drinking tea and eating bread and Vegemite
laughing at the letters of the canisters on the shelf –
Frank Shall Run To Cricket –
and we all break out into that unfamiliar sunlight
where merriment is sublime and the radiance unseasonal
with no need for the kerosene convection heater
with its bootmark still warming odd directions
or the odd number of plates that have somehow survived.
Today is about having survived till today.
About giving thanks.
There is light streaming in
through every window and eye.
Hymns are sung and we resume our seats.
My mother looks to my brother.
He turns to the pulpit where he is standing.
My mother watches as the words grow
into a forest of interconnecting leaves and branches.
And we climb higher, higher, Eugene and I
to get a better view of the scene below
the scene with its tenuous patch of sunlight
dappling in and out of cloud-smothered suburbs.
And we see, we see the places
that can never be the same.
Frog's Hollow. Deepdene. The Emptiness.

Where my father and brother are dressed in white
and my mother in her chair watches over us from the side
and all of the ages of congregations
lift up their eyes to the brilliant white sky
with that look of shock that soon fades
that second when all things are in unison
and are one.

Monk Who Prays So Much He Has Left Footprints Ingrained In the Floor

Time and tide resort to necessities
You'll become so immersed there will be no other
He who prays without expiration
Footprints left ingrained in the floor

You'll become so immersed there will be no other
Every day I come to view the pattern
Footprints left ingrained in the floor
The lines in the soles trace wings in the air

Every day I come to view the pattern
Catching winter respect in the creaking frost
The lines in the soles trace wings in the air
Scriptures shade red the Buddhist elan

Catching winter respect in the creaking frost
Finding courage to step into his footprints
Scriptures shade red the Buddhist elan
Bends down to pray a few thousand times

Finding courage to step into his footprints
Time and tide resort to necessities
Bends down to pray a few thousand times
He who prays without expiration

Time and tide resort to necessities
Footprints left ingrained in the floor
He who prays without expiration
You'll become so immersed there will be no other.

Ways To Approach the Kingdom

How many ways to approach the kingdom?
Registering contacts of another handset?
Gliding beneath green and liberal flotsam?
Counting to one million Facebook friends?
Listening to the wailing of a CFA siren
and waiting for the trucks to scream past?
As Keating once might have been counselled
sitting on a veranda with a baseball bat
waiting for the saviour to arrive?
Watching for the glitz-glam rollover
of the national economic agenda
passed out on the steps of the Acropolis
or drag-racing its own shadow along the Great Wall?
Felling peppercorns down by the dam
so that ordinary identity can be packed into a speedboat
and flung in semi-circles left and right
through the great arcs of Da Vinci's delirium?
Chewing paper under the dome at the State Library
while counting words without vowels?
Loosening the inn from the road
so that merriment breaks out in any informal gathering
even unto the gathering of the self?
Delegating the self to life-long inquiry
into the habits and idiosyncrasies of list-making
or, as Keating might have said
of art in a socially equitable free world
there is no art because it is all art.

Writing lists of those lists until they merge
then blending, grinding or crushing the essences
into a reordering of necessities
creating a sense of creation and creator?
Bending down to retrieve a wafer of truth
that had been walked in attached to a foot?

Cleansing that foot with impure regard?

Fear In a Handful of Dust

I wanna shock you Bethany says
as she unties and lets fall her shoulder-length hair.
She lifts the rifle straight between my eyes.
Repeat after me, coitus strychnine.
What's that I ask.
Go on. Say it.
Coitus strychnine I say slowly as she reasserts her aim
with the heavy hunting rifle nestling further into her armpit.
Kinda gets you excited doesn't it she says.
She lowers the rifle and leads me next door
where the Harbison twins are digging a hole in the lawn
filling it with water then throwing rocks in
the way their dad does at the quarry.
Bethany once again cocks the rifle belonging to my brother
aims it at Kevin and demands
What could you possibly grow in all this rubbish?
I look at her and she leans toward my ear
I'm playing my part, are you? And I wonder
would she one day commit the perfect crime?
None of us would dare surmise.
All I remember is Kevin staring at the water
splashing about the muddy sides
throwing in stones till they disappear
and not looking up, not once.

Wet Salvage Auto Waste

Old Campbell, before his mediaeval philosophies
fell to accents and dialects of barbaric invasion
before dementia derailed remembrance of passing signs
used to work every Saturday in his garage out the back
spot welding the body parts of a living machine.
In the days when a service meant changing your own oil
he was mechanically clockwork every four weeks.
In those days before microchip alienated the know-how
you could hear his low keyed humming in fine tune.
In the days when gears challenged you to a duel at the foot of a hill
or coasting over the hump descending to the valley below
there was no room for the whisper of an automatic transmission.

Old Campbell opened valves by instinct
collecting the sump oil in a tray beneath.
When the last drop had been panned he would brush it
along the next section of fencing
preserving his borders, keeping up appearances.
And peering through knot holes smelling of old engines
he would peruse the plains and the mountains beyond
with their hidden metropolis demystifying out of trees
as farmstead, then hamlet, suburb then satellite
ergonomically pleasing with cars cyber-serviced
and internet-driven along ever-fattening bitumen.
Peering out his eyes caught a melancholy dialect
whether of dog-whelp or of horse breed
or of any of the made-in places
that never provided for his colonial need.
Down streets of cold order in rows of aesthetic
or of the alphabetically sacrificed in an Avenue of Honour.

These were his people toying with hand-honed
with blunt ends of used timber refashioned into usefulness
with limerick, idiom, ballad and adage
and the standard saying since ancestor times
– We get by with what we can do.
No more. For now the grid had multiplied in proportion
in statistical upswings along broadening carriageways
into a matrix from which no one person could escape.
For each time they managed to accelerate and fly free
they were salvaged down the road in the fluids of auto waste.

Old Campbell, one of the many who farmed on their brink
yet joined by a thread down the winding fire tracks
to the hub of the big family below.
Where everyone worked weekdays then on weekends
raffled their time between engines, animal hormones
and the demanded ritual of communal sport.
Where to win was not the goal but involvement with this
people and the next.
Where it mattered enough to the point that newspaper reports
were written about them but only for local readership.
Where at the end of the game there were always scones and beer
beneath dated pennants in the local hall
with bare timber as silent as eucalypt history
as one big family melted into another
with handshakes, songs, bear hugs and laughter.

The unwritten law passed down this way
that competition takes back seat to the spirit of deed
of helping out the likes of Old Campbell
the day his wife dropped at half time
and he had to drive twenty-four miles
to the nearest doctor in his studded boots
both teams forming an armada of speed
to get her there in half the time.
Because even in these parts bereft of reception
people endure even in half measure.

Old Campbell, forgotten in the backwoods of satnav.
Old Campbell, absent-mindedly working silhouettes of his tools.
Finger painting in sump oil and calling her by name.
Old Campbell, at the unwanted heel of Renaissance
cruising his ute down the streets of Cordova
in the century when commonsense was returned by a neighbour
when slowly the town became illuminated, then illumined
and the oil slicked up for its pearl-paved resurrection
Philosophia's bristling wick.

Plum Tree

My mother stands with a spade in her hand.
Time and tide resort to necessities.
She's getting too old for this.
I bring down the mattock again and again
but the earth under the tree is too matted with roots.
Her hair is particularly grey in the hot January sun
and I notice the lines sharpened by concern
that this job will not get finished.
We go inside and drink.
Later in the cool of evening
I continue the futile attempt.
The sunset's fiery orange slides in on our faces
a tint of copper, a countenance of bronze-age
villagers around a community fire.
My mother holds her spade like a weapon.
The lives below us tremble.
So do the sacrifices.

Comfort

I don't like the size of comfort.
It is an unnecessary evil in the architecture of endeavour.
Cities are built for and around it.
People often appear staring at its lazy haze
fobbing off their own purple urban horizon.
Young bodies brown it over a slow heat
in their own definition of the rotating sickie.
Comfort swallows the crowbar mantra
deeper down into earth but without the sudden strike.
Its wedging mallow cushions the ringing nerve
making callous the softer side of a two-tiered society.
Up, down and all around the spires and the towers
immensity of comfort is almost at a premium.
Revolving doors, fast-track flights
ergonomic economics, conferences on skype
a must, a necessity, a nuance over-financed.
But there are some who fit comfort in the flap of a matchcard
squeezing and holding it in a compact treasury
preferring to use it on those who have none –
small, humble, hand-on-a-sleeve enough
to soak up the spirit-essence of any grief
then pinch it into the next minute
but manageable cataclysm.

No Moon Dark

No moon dark.
Even the sparks from the fire are low
each hiding its own separate story.
Even the animals come down to the water hole
in a gulp of nerves following their own footprints.
The tales glance off muffled rock surfaces.
Motifs remain tentative even in this homeland.
A fencepost occasionally withers into view
then is swallowed up by an unforeseen ending.
Fur braces in merging chapters.
Recounts spell shadows in phonetic dialects.
Everywhere the black-ink air
fits like a glove, shatters like a pool.
Everything waits for an unscripted moon
to prowl from the trees
into a flowing narrative.

The Scarred Tree

(In recognition of the Wurundjeri Land and People, Yarra Park)

Linear tendrils spider-weave outward
across this sacred land. Blood of clan
scribbling underwatch beneath trampled clay.
Tyre marks and shoe prints look up
from centuries of light-footed journeys.
Around the scarred tree a circle of women
speak of their ancestry, their clan bond
soaked in that nexus of time and place
where it is defined by animal spirit –
possum, spider, bat, even billabong and stream –
skin and blood flowing with the earth.
To be there is to feel it.
Spirits are engaged by sight and touch.
The women are on an age-old journey
reclaiming a name through sacred witness.
In the wider circle where this tree has lived
thousands have congregated for another religion
with the highs and lows of the external world.
The women know that many of their clans
have been absorbed into racial brotherhood.
There are signs and policies posted everywhere.
Everyone can journey home
following the shouting and the frenzy.
The women believe in this as goodness
but what has it to do with the burnished interior?
They offer silence to the tree
and their veins rankle in its dry heart.

Memory that can't be explained
thrums a long way back from the time
the tree would have risen from seed
in the time of hearing the land's birth cry
the time of good hunting, child-bearing and burial
and the spirit places to the side
and at either end of these
going on, now as then, going on forever
through the time the tree takes
to become its own scar.

Magpie

Being a magpie
I take bits of you
but air, salt and eucalypt
taste more delicious.

Being a magpie
there are silver keepsakes
locked in my armoury
but nothing addresses what we miss
like a hearty melody line.

Being a magpie
I avoid you toying with me
inside a shining opera
but I am not enslaved
and I ascend for no one.

Being a magpie
I am no oracle
in the company of the muse
but with whom would I argue
the reward of music?

Ceremony Poems

1 May-bride

The May-bride circles
about the town
her courtiers looking round
for Whitsun's deadly scythe.
Open your doors
open your doors
for the May-bride to come in.
If you give
you will have plenty.
If you refrain
you will have nothing
and she goes on her merry way
ignoring ghost hands
from the silhouetted she-oaks
targeting the tall blasphemous
figure in the shadows by the lake
whose waters roil
give and take.

2 The Corn Maiden

Who will be the betrothed
draped in inflorescence
of the last harvest?
Oats or wheat

deigned the bridal gown
and the groom's suit of bunches
tied to his arms and legs.
Soon they are boarded

upon a rickety wooden wagon
and towed by two draught horses
to the ale house in the village.
Here they feast and dance

until dawn – that light
of new succour and resurrection –
while the company gradually
remove their clothes

of spike and panicle
and the full rotation
of the seasons' cycles
is reborn in imitation.

3 Photograph of a Bride

What is in the car?
It is the future.

What will breathe in the car
as she alights?
It is the dappled path
through your imagination.

What alights from the car?
It is the raised arm
in the stirred silence.
It is pulsing pillows of air.

What is raised from the car?
It is the arm brushing something
in its imagination and in its future.
It is the air having passed by.
It is the arm of an imminent body.

What is it that stirs in the car?
It is a glimpse, a mere suggestion.
It is the dappled shadow in a photograph
that could never be taken.

At the Homecoming Conference For Philosophers

On the logic of knowledge and belief
spirit and grappa sometimes speak louder than theory.
The Iranian actress was punching holes in the asphalt
and it seemed like a cause and effect line to learn
but only learn. The wishes of her courtiers
made instant success from mythological lashes
right down to the real deal. As the mask
closed its eyes and each scream punctuated blackness
her thoughts wandered to the Theodicean
aspects of Anne Conway's principles –
her flailing mantra – does belief
assume or does it hope? A new
answer to the special composition question
might have triggered the theory of random acts
but it was given by all authority
and those who knew her intimately – the lines
were stuffed and stiffened in her memory –
the way to the mask but a short stroll
through the garden of hope and wild flower existence
where if you sit still long enough
to feel the flesh swell and begin to dream again
you will discover beyond all conditions:
truth arm in arm with a lust for language
shimmying past midnight in the Penguin Bar.

Burying

Eugene says softly
looking down at the scene –
There is no god
because it is all god.

My mother stands with a cross in her hand.
She enters the room where he is laid out.
She returns with a face that is untouched –
reasons masked by a statuesque countenance.

She turns to me to identify him.
She turns away to where I am walking
carrying his coffin.
I am standing alongside her.

We are watching his life
passing by in slow motion.
My mother watches with that wry awry-
lipped accentuation of silence

where nothing is spoken, nor need be
because it has all been done and can pass quietly
through and beneath us.
My mother links what is left to my arm.

She walks gracefully above the earth.
From where we are, everything is in miniature.

The Solitary Boat

At evening
on the rippling waters
the lapping side to side motion
of a solitary boat.
No oars, no rudder
it sits atop the fluid spaciousness
as a thought, or in thought
knowing it would not exist
but for the water
in its shallows and in its depths.
And from above, the boat is lit
by a ray of sunlight
breaking between the clouds
and here too, another thought
comes to mind –
its knowledge of balance
within and between
great and gentle forces.
The boat is allowed
to go this way forever.
For the people in the village
tending their nets or
just watching from the shore
the solitary boat reflects
great happiness and sorrow.
They know they will be carried
when the waters receive them.

The Painting

The painting in the attic
was a prisoner of its own immunity.
Given the chance to escape under some wily arm
it would have inflated like a blow-up dollar
and rained down upon the patronising aristocracy.
Within its myriad spectral daubs
hairline blacks could be seen bleeding into shadows.
The painting in the attic
depicted something acquiring dying rapture.
It sounded like the strings of rainfall
gently cascading to the rooftops below.
It smelt of wet earth just after a storm
and it tasted of salt rising to the skin.
The painting in the attic
depicted something cutting loose a rapture dying.
It felt like a hand passing through its own grasp
gristled and rutted with every demonstrative stroke
up, across then down
the shadow within the darkness
the attic in the painting.

Terra Momentum

Rumours and tales fell adrift
rippling and swaying every square inch of skin
and hectare across the entire state.
Cockatoos bumped on the road.
Old Holdens lurched into a new gear.
Rocks and stones elevated, floated, then put down
metres from where they had crept for centuries.
Kelp wrapped anchors' gravitational sway
with odd-looking kraken and Neptune finery.
Oil rigs buckled at the knees
screaming blue flames with nowhere to hide.
Gippsland thought about moving south.
Neighbours slept side by side on beaches
or behind walls, guessed at strongly-dealt intercourse
beyond acceptable Richter standards.
Indeed, for a while, the whole bonk bonk
of the tectonic resistance resembled
intricate libraries with their books spilled out
records obliterated, then the crystal all smashed
so that readings of anything above five would be felt
around campfires beside lakes that were no longer lakes –
anecdotal, representational, a serious ritual
where you can be accepted by the fates
of earth moving for you
or a roof caving in
or stay steady enough to tell
in the Trafalgar Hotel
how you feared for your life
plural and ditto
the same horror motto

up the ranges to Bright
and across to the Mallee
as if shaken from three decades
of oblivious sex, but without
ever knowing the epicentre.

Growing Old

The legacy of being old enough to die
is carved silently into waiting room after waiting room.
Old jokes grow older for Gen New
and old tricks cramp in the presence of double-jointedness.
Sale on instant similes, shortcuts flat-screened onto carry-on wafer pads
instant generated philosophies degenerating as they switch on.
Aged and aging telemarketing on every billboard
behaving like an oxymoron in the best possible protocol
and the next to be called –
number one –
what will it be today?
The ultrasound is alerted with greased-up precision
over the floweret of a whole internal organ
swaying in black misnomers
benign this time
but carved in the memory.

Mutating Contours of a Lime Sea

You're dreaming of those nights when, neither here nor there
you are dreaming inside the dream of sleep slipping away
and with it the anchored nerve standing on the shore
anxiously wringing its jittery limbs
as it begins to drift like kelp adroit
secretly drowning for a deeper vista
within its sea of touch out of reach.
Here, the coastal mourners implore
even at the turning of the tide
the solitary boat arriving.
'Come with us now, for ebb tide is upon us
and we must depart for that farthest land.'
Slowly, here or there, your limbs fade to transparency.
Through listless hands coral and water music
bleed their colours into your own
until you can barely manage to see yourself
and the texture grows around you
like an ocean swallowing
its own salty void.

A Long, Low-sweeping Pastoral Sadness

Sunlight oiled on every sinew and limb
his name the rule of thumb of naming
boys and men from whence their fathers came
and his father before that, almost as if desirable
to confuse the family name with its countryside.
Not so the cattle and the brand, sweeping down
from the high hills all the way to his arm
the chaff-filtered light from the first star
older and truer than any familiar person or place.
He knew too well, in too many eyes
of sentenced beasts, the ring of gold light like life
seen often from his veranda, coming round again
for everyone born under this star, this family name
fulfilled, like an infant first saying it, like destiny.

Destiny was strong, sweaty under a flannelled arm
could walk into a room, pick you up by the eyes
shake the fear into you, attach you to dry horror
then, wider and warmer than Carpentaria, smile you off-balance
or on one arm lift a whole new generation
green and screeching with parrot nerves
high and fear-swept, laying it down peacefully
again – not this time my children.

Rising each morning under a wisp of desultory
eddying between his toes and fingers
with ferret litheness, the crannies and gullies of
an adopted fatherland, his Sunday chantings
along the hymnal divide, the brimstone cleavages
of quartz faith, rabbit-warren ill-luck
hollowed inhuman decay and shale shard
as thick and solid as an axeman's forearm.
He nevertheless rose flimsily on a dream of knowledge
from the resounding ocean of more than forty thousand years
which had inhabited his land with spirits, narguns
low whistlings, kite shriekings, rhythms and burnishings
a spirit of reality he would never understand
for another forty thousand of God-fearing inheritance.

Now travelling down the bending arm of the Murray
past listless campers surfacing for the heat of day
the caravans, the tents, the campervans, trailers
body-boards, jet-skis, totem tennis and beer.
The full load of summer shimmers in the haze
as the skiers tilt their frames to the gradient
of forest embankments with unherded cattle
and gnarled eucalypts of the dreaming census.

And farther back, upstream, where the lagoons rise in the off
season
where ibis shun the holiday sheen for worthless carp
and the shadows mottle on long-gone campsites
the yellow-green of faded tent floors, cigarettes, open tins
the charcoal, the bottles, all along the fading line, stream of
evolution
evidence and implements of a failed species.
The river tells it all, stays true to its aim
and leaves its mark on the land the way a land should receive life.

It was here he had come to and from, at a point in his life
where he was still and stagnant, because somewhere the silt and
the salt
somewhere where estuary espies its source, as death's own
standstill, still standing
the eucalypt trick of stillness, that gold ring of light
of stretched canvas yawning over a whole culture
blind to what is really true in this land of banksia, goanna
bush fly, termite or European wasp, because somewhere the silt
and the salt
steady in the eye of tree and storm, in the eye and tree of man
still land, still life, a dark secret too lucid to be caught alive
unable to be said, but can be felt, unable to move, but can run
through your fingers.
He had come here with those canvasses stretched across his eyes
for forty-three years and names, Streeton, Boyd, McCubbin,
Roberts
peeled off him like snake-skin as he saw what they saw –
the true still eye of the eucalypt's reflection.

It was here he had come to and from, to a fork in the river
to where memory and place have no place or memory
and he looked no farther – the gold ring of trees at day's end
captured some spark still left in his eye
to seek out someone from somewhere again.

Filling the Gaps

They brought trucks around night and day.
We watched from the railing on top of the overpass.
We watched them filling it in
with shale and grit from a quarry somewhere.
Palls of nightmarish similes
steamed from caved-in mouths in the ground
and from our own fractious visions
the future was dragged in slow motion
to the level of our eyes.
Archie the Wimmera farmer.
Eugene who went to Canada for good.
The man on the overpass who didn't really see anyone.
Bethany the actress who died from the perfect dose.
All of us drift back and forth
from and toward and over the bridge.
We watch them put something in a box
made of human-shaped euphemisms
of their own choosing.
We never look up.
Not once.

The Immensity

(with reference to the film *Mr Ibrahim and the Flowers of the Koran*)

I met a man who lived inside a movie.
He only breathed in its flickering shadows
and although his life was a constant repetition
he held the key perhaps without even knowing it
and he always smiled.

I met this man just the other night
and in our conversation he told me an important truth
and I admitted to him an embarrassing distortion.

You see, some people never return from the emptiness
and emptiness, smoothed over, cannot hide immensity

and this is where

> *Dear Reader*
> *We leave this poem for a while. We stand to the side of it.*
> *Because somebody has passed. Like so many visions back*
> *then, seen from a railing or a fence, euphorias that cannot*
> *be touched, but are seen, fading before they materialise. The*
> *body, immense, already elevated and the emptiness it leaves*
> *behind, worldly. Bethany leans into my ear – There is no*
> *performance because it is all a performance.*

(At this point, pure silence.)

Outside the movie over coffee in a bar, I asked him
'Where do you go if you step outside of poetry
if you step outside of prayer where do you go?'

He smiled at me.
'It is a word – like sublime, silesh, shantih –
I cannot speak it yet for my time is not yet here.'

And with that, he tipped his cap and walked off into the Immensity.
And with all due respect these lines belong in a film.
And with all due respect the audience could not distort them.
The audience, to a person, left smiling, knowing nothing.

Farmhouse

Before dawn
all over the dark paddocks
long silken threads quiver

a metallic blue
seeps below the black sky
down near the horizon.

In the kitchen
he is shadow, he is formless
his children still asleep
in a questioning tangle of limbs
their weights fitfully spread
between the shared mattress
and the clutching of fingers
at the end of dreams.

With the flick of his forefinger
buttermilk light, Osram sixty-watt
spills over the window ledge
melts into the yard
and across the fields
where black ice bleeds green
and into the shank of the brittle night
where it can be seen
over hillocks and mountains
from the nearest star
seen as a dish of gold pour
glowing unwanted in the sunken retreats
of bush people overwhelmed
by the power pole plantations.

But the light is slow this morning
it struggles, its element flickers
at something out there, its syrupy floe
grates and greases across jigged stones
the light that creeps into every corner
cutting short along the track to the barn
where the blood-red door dilutes to mauve
and the eye of rabbit or fox
sometimes fluoresces along the journey
the light still fanning down to the yards
with the stillness of cattle stirring with milk
snaking under the mulberry bush shadow
slowing as if warned, slipping over
the slim mound
then out into hawk sky
entangling with an evil
that won't go away.

His fingers as numb
as the day's first milking
life syphoning back life
as soft as blood
as he clutches, releases
the hot stream of his living
her touch the first time
all night to her bosom
the years, the centuries
that seemed to pass
before progress thundered
in from the plains.

In the farmhouse
small light
in the middle of nowhere
his hand on the switch
his mind on the lever
all that immensity
all that darkness
and the mystery of children.
The light thins as dawn rises.
Soon his children will awaken
to the cold light of day
and his hands release
from their grip on the land
the things that can
never be the same.

www.ingramcontent.com/pod-product-compliance
Lightning Source LLC
Chambersburg PA
CBHW062152100526
44589CB00014B/1800